Beyond the Shadows

Beyond the Shadows

FREEDOM TO EMBRACE THE LIGHT WITHIN

Emily Hayes

Editor/Paul James

Forward by Dr. Raynia L. McGee

Cover Design by jeweldsign

Cover photography by Jessica Latten

ISBN 978-1-0991-6123-0 (paperback)

*To the beautiful spirit who has blessed this place
and changed the world,
Your life has been a blessing to the lives of many,
and I thank you for who you are, what you do, and the
love you give. Although this life comes with its
challenges, you always find it in you to wake up and
face each day with courage, strength and resilience.
No other compares to you. Continue to love boldly.
Continue to laugh loudly. Continue to live freely. I am
grateful for you every day, and without you there
would be no reason for my light to shine.
I dedicate this book to you.*

Table of Contents

Forward

What brings you in to see me today? As a physician, every day I see patients who are searching for an answer to a medical question. Why am I in pain? Why can't I sleep? Is this disease terminal? Will this medication work? In today's society, people are now asking additional questions regarding purpose, emotional health, acceptance of self, and authenticity. Does my life matter? How can I make a difference in the world? What does it mean to be happy? Will I ever feel complete?

For the past ten years, I have watched the author of this book as she searched for answers to her own questions of self-worth and purpose. Through the wisdom of her own experiences and formal education, she shares concrete and practical steps to help readers reach their full potential. This book does not provide overly simplistic and "pat" answers. The path to self-awareness and self-acceptance is a difficult one. It is a path lined with periods of self-doubt, unrealistic expectations, mistakes, and failures. However, for those who have the courage to stay the course and move through the dark times, the path can be exhilarating. Walking into the light of personal truth can be miraculous, humbling and full of tangible and intangible gifts.

I encourage readers to gather your most sacred questions and fears and begin the journey toward reaching your full potential. In this book, you will learn to honor the person you were and who you are. In addition, you will learn how to move into the light of who you can be. You will learn how to make progress that is sustainable and life-altering. Take the first step, move out of the darkness and into the light, for that is where greatness thrives.

Journeying with you in great expectation of what can be,

Raynia L. McGee, M.D.

Preface

Many people have expressed that my spirit and energy bring them joy when I'm in their presence. I love being the reason for someone's smile. I love being the flame that sparks someone's joy. I love when my presence is an uplifting gift to others. I am a giver. For those who know me, know that it is difficult for me not to want to give. As I was having a conversation with a good friend, it was explained to me that I have a lot to offer the world. However, if I'm not willing to overlook my momentary feelings of discomfort and focus on the bigger picture, then I'm preventing myself from living out my purpose. It's easy to center the decisions I make around my feelings, especially when those feelings are undesirable. But life is full of undesirable feelings. These feelings are called growth. These feelings are called experience. I had to accept that what others needed from me was more important than the temporary feelings of discomfort. In accepting that, I came to realize that when I embrace the experience, when I embrace the growth, and when I embrace the discomfort, I am able to present a better version of myself to others because I understand it is all working for my good. I have something special that needs to be shared with you, and I can't share that if I'm constantly running away from the things that make me uncomfortable. The idea of this book came to me as I was sitting at work one morning, writing my daily entry in my journal. After writing in my journal, I began sending out my weekly inspiring text messages. I loved the idea of being able to encourage people with positive messages. I then asked myself how I could share what I have to offer with others. How could I have a positive impact on more lives? How could I inspire more people? The answer... write a book. I have a deep desire to help others in whatever capacity I can. There are many great books that have been written to inspire the reader to do or feel something creative. My desire is to inspire you to discover your greatness by freeing yourself from the things that may be hindering you from living out your purpose.

Beyond the Shadows

FREEDOM TO EMBRACE THE LIGHT WITHIN

Emily Hayes

INTRODUCTION

Who are you? Most answers to this question either involve us telling people our name (family origin) and what we do for a living, or we describe ourselves using our physical characteristics. But do you truly know who you are? Have you ever thought about who you are? Are you able to answer this question without using your name, physical characteristics or your occupation? Would you like to know who I am? I am a spiritual being with unlimited power. I am a source of life. I am a divine light. I am a gift to the world. You too are a gift. Each of us was created with a unique purpose embedded inside of us. Each of us was created with special gifts that bring light to this world in their own special way.

Often times we lurk in the shadows of inadequacy. We've convinced ourselves that who we are or what we have to offer isn't good enough. We've wrapped ourselves in so many layers of fear that we've lost sight of our truth. The truth is, we are all spiritual beings with unlimited power. But in order for that to be your truth, you have to believe that you are important and believe greatness manifests from within you. When you become knowledgeable of self you realize your self-worth. It is important to know that you are valuable. It is equally important to know that you are mortal, and you have a limited amount of time in your physical body. Therefore, strive to live each day in your purpose and not just constricted by your

3

obligations. When we don't see our value, we become victims of life instead of creators of life. Is life happening to you or from you? Are you creating your life or are you merely existing within the limitations you've placed on yourself and the expectations others have placed on you?

I wrote Beyond the Shadows to remind some and make others aware that they are light and their gift is the pathway to freedom. We lose sight of our own purpose when we focus our energy and attention on chasing after another person's dreams. We let the expectations of society dictate how we live our life. We let the fear of the unknown hinder us from walking in our purpose and dancing in our passion. Choosing a life of freedom means choosing a life of truth... your truth. When we step beyond our shadows (outside of our comfort zones) we expose ourselves to a world of possibilities, a world of peace, love and joy, a world of freedom. I hope this book inspires you to discover what freedom means to you, gain the courage to break free from your perceived limitations and live a life full of experience and purpose. You are a light in this world, and you were created to shine in your greatness.

GREATNESS CAN'T SHINE IN THE SHADOWS

"Shine bright like a diamond" – Rhianna

I will be a doctor! You will be what? I will be a doctor! No one in your family graduated high school. What makes you think YOU, of all people, have what it takes to be a doctor?

I will write a book! You can't write a book. You don't know the first thing about writing a book. What are you going to talk about? I have a lot of things to talk about. No one cares what you have to say.

I will start my very own business! What do you know about owning a business? Don't most new business fail within the first three years of starting? That could be true, but that doesn't mean mine will fail. I know that I have a gift, and I will use my gift to serve others. Yeah. That all sounds good, but what happens when you fail and you aren't able to "serve" your bills with this so-called gift?

Isn't it funny how we can be our own worst enemies? As one of my favorite clients would often say, "not funny, ha ha but funny, peculiar". Of course, it's not funny that we can be our own worst enemies, but most times it is definitely true. The world is full of enough negative energy, naysayers, negative thinkers, and negative opinions without us adding to that pot of self-defeating gumbo. When was the last time you contemplated doing something you thought was awesome, and you let someone else talk you out of it? When was the last time you contemplated doing something awesome, and you let yourself talk you out of it? When was the last time someone told you that you would be great at doing something, and you didn't think you were good enough to even try it, let alone be great at it? Oh, so I'm the only one who has been there? Well, since you don't want to taste your gumbo, let me give you a taste of mine. I've been eating this gumbo for years. I didn't grow up in a rough neighborhood. I didn't go to a school with a poor success rate. I didn't have people whispering in my ear telling me I would never amount to anything. I didn't look out the classroom window and see unemployed people hanging out on the steps of the projects. I didn't have to sleep on the floor at night because of constant gunfire. I didn't have to share a bed with my siblings. I didn't have people pressuring me to do or sell drugs. Let's be clear about something. I'm not making these statements to make anyone feel bad, inadequate, or less of a person. I'm making these statements to show that even if you grow up in a positive environment, with a strong support system, there are still challenges to be faced, and most times, the challenges faced are the ones we place on ourselves. My parents, my family, my friends, my church members, my classmates, my coaches, my teachers, basically most of the people in my life have always believed in me. My family has always supported me and cheered me on in everything I did. From tap dancing (well, I think that was more of Mom's decision. Love you Mom) to creating my custom line of hand-painted jewelry and writing this book. I've experienced a lot in life, as we all have. I've also missed out on a lot of exciting opportunities because I kept eating that doggone self-defeating gumbo. I grew up listening to my dad telling me that I can use my talents to start my own business. I would usually just brush those comments off. He told me I could play in the WNBA. He told me I could have a business selling diaper cakes. He told me I could write my own cookbook. He told me I could open my own restaurants. Basically, anything I did or tried doing, my dad believed I could be great at it. He could watch me do one thing, and he envisioned me doing it on a much larger scale. I didn't even have to be halfway decent at it, and he would still believe in me. From soccer goalie and scrapbooking to baby wreaths and hand painted jewelry, my dad has always seen the greatest of possibilities. I, on the other hand, tended to think more about why I couldn't be successful at any of those things. I didn't believe in myself. I didn't think I was good enough to excel in whatever it was I was doing. I realize now that all of those negative thoughts and all of that self-doubt came from me focusing my attention on what others had done. It's quite difficult to be great at something and to see greatness in yourself when you're using most of your time and energy comparing your uniqueness to others. Think about it. How are you able to discover your own greatness when the majority of your time is spent convincing yourself that what you have to offer or what you created doesn't look, sound, or feel the way someone else's creations do? My dad looked at me, and he saw a fountain of limitless possibilities, but for some reason, all I could see were my limitations. That reason is because I used more energy admiring how other people did things and telling myself the way I did it wasn't as good as the way they did it. Instead, I should have been telling myself that I could do things in my own unique way just as well as they did those things in their own unique way. I didn't believe in myself. I have no idea where my mental block came from, but I can say for certain that it has prevented me from doing a lot of great things in my earlier years. Believing in myself was like trying to win American Ninja Warrior. I knew there was a finish line. I knew there was a way to get to it successfully. I had just as good of an opportunity to win as the next person, but I didn't believe it. Somewhere between that first obstacle and the 14 foot 6-inch warped wall, I would defeat myself. I lost the race before it had even begun. I know now that the only existing limitations are the ones we place on ourselves. By the way, if you've never watched American Ninja Warrior, you should! It's a great example of how we should live. It reminds us that even though something may seem crazy, too hard or absolutely impossible at first glance, it never is. There's no difference between the people who choose to compete in American Ninja Warrior and the people who choose to compete in life. Some of us see a mountain and decide to stay where we are or turn back around. Others see a mountain and begin brainstorming on solutions to get over it, around it or through it. We all have mountains, but I've come to realize that most of life's mountains are self-constructed. What's more, many of our mountains are only perceived as mountains because we don't know how to embrace the adventures and experiences of life. Instead, we allow our fear of the unknown, our fear of failure or even our fear of success to lead us into thinking we aren't good enough to get to the other side. However, once we realize that we have all the creative power in the world, we will understand that we have the power to demolish those mountains. Is this gumbo starting to taste familiar now? Some of you had a great support system but just couldn't seem to wrap your mind around the idea of you being good enough despite what others told you. Some of you had a small support system, and you believed you were good enough in some situations but not others. Some of you, regardless of how big or small your support system is or was, have never believed you were good enough to act on your dreams, and there's a possibility you still don't. I'm here to tell you that you are the next American Ninja Warrior!! Okay okay, maybe that's a bit much, but you are good enough! Everything you are is good enough! Everything you have to offer is good enough! There is greatness inside of you that you were born with, and it's waiting for you to release it. If you don't believe me, just keep reading. Side note, if you've always believed in yourself, kudos to you for embracing your greatness and letting your light shine.

We are all given opportunities in life to explore our unique light, but it's up to us to nurture and embrace the thing(s) that makes us great, the things that help us shine. Why are you afraid to embrace your greatness? Do you know what it is that you possess that makes you great? Are you afraid of the unknown? Are you afraid you'll fail? Are you afraid you'll succeed? Are you afraid to come from behind your mountains and live a life beyond the shadows? I am definitely someone who has been afraid to step beyond the shadows. For most of my life, I operated in the shadows. I'm not talking about the physical shadows; I'm talking about my personal shadows. What if I told you that the shadows I speak of are commonly known as our comfort zone? Does that shift your view on this conversation? My shadows were my insecurities and fears. I had things about myself that I've been insecure about. Let's get real transparent here for a second. I had a conversation with my little cousin one day about embracing and loving every part of yourself, especially the things that other people might make fun of. One of my insecurities was my feet. I have long, flat, narrow feet and long toes. I didn't know my toes were long until other people with shorter toes pointed it out. See how other people's opinions can change the way you view yourself? Okay, I have long toes, well guess what, if I drop the washcloth in the shower, I can use my long toes to grab it and pick it up without having to bend all the way over and risk water running up my neck and into my ears. I used to bury my feet in the sand when I was on the beach because of my toes and the bunion on my left foot. Well, my foot, my long toes and my bunion have played sports, have taught dance classes, and have traveled to different countries and so many other things. One of the most recent insecurities I've overcome were my grey hairs. I used to be embarrassed because my hairs were starting to turn grey in my twenties. I began to cut them because I didn't want people to comment about me going grey at my age. I didn't want to hear "why are you going grey you're so young?" Heck! I don't know why my hair is turning grey. Am I supposed to provide the answer to that question? I no longer cut my grey hairs, I embrace them. And yes I still get comments and questions about having grey hairs at my age, but it doesn't bother me anymore. That mountain was something I constructed and decided to destroy. Not to mention, I have a patch of grey hairs in the front of my head that, once they grow all the way out, I'm going to look like I should be the newest member of The Avengers.

Do you have any physical differences that have you feeling insecure about yourself? If so, I encourage you to acknowledge them and find out why you feel insecure about them. Then, understand that your differences are good. Your differences may actually be an avenue that will allow others to relate to you and may result in your light being an inspiration to them.

Okay Emily, you have skeleton feet and grey hair. What's the big deal? That's just it, it shouldn't be a big deal. Most of the things we mold into becoming big deals to us are insignificant in the grand scheme of things. We're focused on the tiny specs of dust on the car windshield, and it's causing us to completely miss our exits. For example, I have a phobia of public speaking. Ever since I was a child, I never liked speaking in front of people. The church, the classroom, the family get-togethers, it didn't matter. If

I was required to speak in front of a group of people, big or small, and all eyes were on me, I hated it. I would get nervous. My armpits would start sweating uncontrollably, my face would turn red, my voice would shake, and my lips would tremble. I have yet to figure out what it is, but it still happens to this day. The difference between then and now is, I have come to understand that I am here for a reason, and regardless of what physical limitations I place on myself and what fears I choose to feed, there is something inside of me that needs to be shared because people like you need to hear it, see it, and experience it. What good is a light bulb if it stays in the box? What if a light bulb said: "You know what, I don't want to come out. I'm shaped funny. My box isn't as good as the other light bulbs' boxes. The ink printed on me isn't clear enough for people to read it. I'm only a 40-watt light bulb. I might as well stay in my box for the rest of my shelf life." That light bulb was created for a purpose, yet it focused on its own self-doubt, insecurities, and fears to prevent it from gifting its light to others. It's the same for me and you. You are a light. You have talents and gifts that need to be shared with the world, but you're allowing your tiny windshield specs and what other people MIGHT think to keep you in the shadows. A few years ago, I started a non-profit organization. I wanted the non-profit to be faceless. I wanted people to acknowledge the things we were doing more than the person doing them. I didn't want to be on camera. I didn't want to speak in front of crowds. I wanted to stay in the shadows hoping that somehow the service we provided would speak for itself and people would miraculously donate and sponsor us. My friends were constantly telling me I needed to show my face. It wasn't so that I could get the praise, but it was so others could feel a connection. Opening up and allowing that potential connection could result in people being more inclined to help when an opportunity to donate or volunteer became available, but because I was so focused on the spec (myself) I missed my exit. I missed the fact that being relatable could actually benefit the organization and the people we serve. One afternoon, I was having a conversation with a friend, and it was brought to my attention that everything I said I didn't want to happen was happening and it was because of me. Hold up! You mean to tell me, this entire time I'm hiding in the shadows wanting to keep the attention off of me, and I'm the one who's directing more attention to my fears and excuses than towards the people. Wow! Talk about checks and balances. I was more concerned with my discomfort than I was with the potential to reach more people and have a bigger positive impact on the world. I was hiding my light in the shadows because I didn't like the feeling of discomfort. As a result, the people in the world who need my light are getting a dim version or aren't getting it at all.

What gifts and talents are you hiding in the shadows because you're more afraid of experiencing momentary discomfort? What greatness are you keeping to yourself because you're more concerned with what other people might think than you are with how your light will help others? We were born with a custom made greatness. We each have different gifts, talents, and abilities that are unique. When we acknowledge that we're great, embrace our uniqueness and act on it, we begin to let our light shine. We tend to forget that life has an expiration date on it. Our time on this earth is limited. Why do we focus on the tiny specs? Why are we so comfortable letting the opinions of others dictate whether or not we express our gifts and walk in our purpose? Maya Angelou said it best, "There is no greater agony than burying an untold story inside of you."

You should know that you are a vessel carrying a very important gift. Take a moment to think about where you are and what you're doing in this stage of your life. Now, take a moment to think about where you could be and what you could be doing if you stepped beyond the shadows (your comfort zone) and embraced your light within. How different would your life be? How would your impact on the people around you change? How would changing your impact on those people result in changing the world?

YOU ARE IMPORTANT

"How is not living in your purpose impacting someone else?" –
Dr. Myles Munroe

You are here because you have a purpose. Everything that has ever been created was created with a specific purpose in mind. Planes were created so that we can fly. Washing machines were created to wash clothes. Chairs were created so that we would have something more comfortable to sit on. Boxes were created to store things. Bags were created to carry things. You are no different. You were created with a purpose, and you have an internal instruction manual that will guide you to not only finding your purpose but fulfilling it as well. Many of us don't know what our purpose is in life or how to find it. To quote author and transformational coach Joe Burnett: "Your gift will always touch the soul or spirit of a person".

This is why you are important. You possess a gift that when shared with others will touch the spirit of them the way no one else will. There are thousands of inspiring stories. There are thousands of singers and dancers. There are thousands of motivational speakers. There are thousands of entertainers. And there are thousands of inspirational books. Each of them has a way of touching the spirit of people the way the others do not. To discover your purpose, you must be willing to look inside yourself.

It took me about 10 years to discover my purpose. I wasn't intentionally looking for it. Actually, I wasn't looking for it at all, I was one of those people walking around wondering what I would do in life but never really took the initiative to find the answer to that question. I was comfortable enough with not knowing because after all, I was at least doing something. It's almost as if I subconsciously thought that my purpose in life would show up one day and find me, instead of me seeking it. That's not how it works. Many of us believe that just doing something is good enough. We go to work. We tend to our families. We pay our bills on time. We pick up a side job or two to keep us busy. But even with all that, we still aren't seeing our worth. We still aren't living out the purpose we were born with. We tend to think that a lot of movement equates to progress and productivity. We spend our lives on a treadmill running in place but going nowhere. Sure we feel accomplished because we're moving, but what good is movement in life without direction? Here's how I came to discover my purpose. I realize now that the journey to discovering my purpose didn't begin until I started using my gifts. As I was pursuing my undergraduate degree, part of my course plan required me to take courses that taught me how to instruct group fitness classes. Not everyone taking the courses with me enjoyed the thought of instructing a class or even being in group fitness classes but for me, it was exciting and fun. Those courses and instructors opened the door and exposed me to things I had never considered before. Not long after taking those courses, I obtained a group fitness certification, and I fell in love with teaching group fitness classes. I always feel so energized after teaching a class. Knowing that the routines, something I created, make people feel good and help them become a happier healthier version of themselves brings me joy. In August 2015 I created my own group fitness class, and I named it SERVED. By the end of the year, I had set aside a couple hundred dollars from teaching the classes. I considered saving the money, but then I realized that there were people in the world who needed the money more than I. So I found a way to use the money from the SERVED group fitness classes to give back to the community. I wasn't sure how when or where I would do this, but I knew it was something I wanted to do, and I knew someone needed me to do it.

Fast forward to January 2016, I remember sitting in the parking lot of my job looking up what I thought were random scriptures. I came across 1 Peter 4:10, and as soon as I read the verse I knew it was meant for me. The Scripture reads "each of you should use whatever gifts you have received to serve others..." As soon as I read it, my spirit light flickered inside of me and that moment revealed to me why I saved the money from the SERVED classes. Later that year I organized and hosted my first successful community service project. The level of joy I experienced from being able to serve so many people from the very building where I began teaching my classes was immeasurable. I never knew what I truly wanted to do in life until that experience. My purpose is to serve and bring joy to others. My life goal is to inspire millions. Your purpose can be found in your gifts, but you have to be willing to explore them. You have to realize that you are important, and there is something you have that the world needs. Do you know what your gifts are? Have you ever considered using your gifts to be of service to others? Looking at your gifts, the things you're good at, and the things you enjoy doing is a great place to start when beginning the journey of discovering your purpose. What are some things you are good at and enjoy doing? How can you use what you're good at to serve others?

The value of anything is not determined by where it is or isn't located, nor is it determined by how many people experience it. The value of anything in life is determined by the person who possesses it or desires to possess it. A cardboard box that once held a refrigerator may not be valuable to the person who purchased the refrigerator, but to a homeless person living on the streets, it holds much value. The same box discarded as trash after its contents had been removed is also the same box picked up and treated as a treasure. What once was used simply as a carrying case for an inanimate object is now protecting life or lives from being directly exposed to rains, winds, snow, freezing temperatures, etc. When you know who you are, when you know your purpose, when you know your value, nothing can be said or done to you to make you question any of those things. When you arrive at that mountain top in your life, you arrive at a place of peace. You're okay with the fact that not everyone will accept you, not everyone will value you, not everyone will see your worth, and that's when you dig your roots deeper into the soil of your self- worth and continue to soak up all of your divine nutrients. You shouldn't waste your time trying to please people who don't recognize your value, and you shouldn't waste your time trying to convince anyone that you are valuable. The tree doesn't stop growing because someone cuts it down, and neither should you. It's likely that you've seen the pictures of a stump with a small sprout proudly standing as tall as it can in the middle of the stump. Maybe you've even been blessed enough to see it in person. As long as the tree still has roots, it will continue to reach towards the sun. Trees are valuable to ALL life, but not everyone recognizes their value or cares to acknowledge it. Many companies cut down trees because they want more space to build cold, lifeless buildings. People cut down trees because they're tired of raking leaves in the fall. Trees are our source of oxygen. Anything that breathes oxygen relies on trees to survive. Trees are homes to many creatures. Trees are our shade. How many times do you drive to work looking for a parking space beneath a tree to keep your car shaded while you work inside of a building for 8-12 hours? You may not consciously think about it, but you value that tree for what it can provide for you. The tree does not stop giving off oxygen, it does not stop being a home to other creatures, it does not stop providing shade or shelter just because someone walks by it and says it's in the way, it's dropping too many leaves on the ground, it's blocking their view of other buildings, and so on. The tree, without shame, fear, or doubt, continues to live its life, and it continues to operate in the purpose for which it was created. Likewise, you must be bold enough to stand tall and live out your purpose by operating in your gifts. It is imperative that you remember external opinions do not have the power to alter internal value/worth. When you know who you are, when you know your value, and when you know your purpose, the words of others will never be powerful enough to take that away from you. You possess the same power in your thoughts, in your words, and in your beliefs. The same amount of energy it requires to ponder negative thoughts is the same amount of energy used to dance about in positive thinking. It is up to you to decide which will be more beneficial to you and the lives of others.

You have to value yourself and know your worth. Stand firm in your beliefs, because if you believe you're valuable then eventually someone else will believe you're valuable. You must realize that once you believe it, you will see it. You can't wait until you see it to believe it. You should not believe everything you see with the physical eye. You must first start believing it, and you must continue to believe it long enough until you begin to see it. Eventually, others will begin to see your value. Muhammad Ali wasn't the greatest when he started boxing, but he believed he was the greatest and continued to believe he was the greatest. Not only did he think and believe he was the greatest, but he spoke that he was the greatest. Many people thought he was crazy for shouting "I'm the greatest!" as he ran up and down the streets, but Muhammad Ali saw his value. Imagine if he would've listened to all the negative criticism, doubters, and people calling him a fool for making claim to being the greatest. The same power Ali had is the same power within you. You have the same power to remain optimistic and believe in yourself. Because Ali believed he was the greatest, we now have people purchasing posters, mugs, t-shirts, paintings, etc. with pictures of Muhammed Ali on them. People are now quoting the same phrases he spoke as he was emitting energy into the universe and believing he was the greatest. Muhammad Ali is an inspiration and a motivation to many. People value his achievements and work because he believed he was valuable, not because he relied on other people to show him he was valuable. He continued to believe it because he could see it before it came to be, and soon people began to see it and believe it for themselves too. Realize that what you have inside of you is the power to do and be anything you want. The only way you can lose that power is if you give it away. The only way you can lose the belief in your value and self - worth is if you give it up. No one can take away your value, and no one can take away your power to have an optimistic outlook. This isn't Space Jam. The Nerdlucks can't touch you and your power automatically be extracted from your body. Sure, someone can touch you and feel/absorb your energy just as you can feel/absorb someone else's energy, but it can't be taken from you or vice versa. You have to make a conscious choice to stop being positive and recognizing your self -worth. Allowing outside noise to drown out your melody of hope and positivity can prevent you from achieving your greatest accomplishments. Look inside yourself and continuously seek that buried gem. You have to believe in yourself, your ideas, your dreams, your mission, your goals, and your passion with an unquestionable faith. When you realize your value and believe in yourself long enough, you'll begin to physically see yourself becoming all that you ever imagined you could be.

When was the last time you've stood in front of the mirror and looked inside of yourself? Pay close attention to that question. Notice I said looked inside of yourself and not looked at yourself. Our outside is just a shell carrying the spirit that resides within. When we take time to look beyond the shell, we realize that there's something more nourishing to be observed and experienced. If it weren't for marine biologists, we wouldn't know a fraction of the creatures that exist beneath the surface of the ocean. You too are like an ocean. You have a penetrable surface, but deep beyond the crests of your waves is a greatness, and for some of you, this greatness has yet to be discovered. Everything on this planet depends on something else in order for it to exist. Nothing can continue to exist on its own. The rain can't exist without the rivers, lakes or oceans. Likewise, the rivers, lakes, and oceans can't exist without the rain. People can't exist without the flowers, plants, and trees giving us oxygen, and the flowers, plants, and trees can't exist without something giving them carbon dioxide. These relationships aren't always at the forefront of our minds, but we live on a planet where other people and other things depend on one another for survival. Every decision you make has consequences. Your decisions have a ripple effect on the people, places, and things around you. When you went out to lunch with your coworkers today instead of eating the leftovers from last night's meal, your decision had several consequences. You spent money today that you had not planned on spending. You may have met someone while you were out that you wouldn't have encountered by staying in the office. Your car being on the road could've caused someone else to get stuck at a red light. I could go on, but you get the idea. Every decision you make always impacts someone or something else, with or without your knowledge. That is why it is important to understand that you are important. Without your decisions, many things may not exist in the manner that they do as a result of your decisions. If you don't realize your impact and your importance, then the world will miss out on the great things that are within you. With that being said it is imperative that we do not allow the opinions of others to influence our self-worth or define our level of importance. Take a moment to perform a self-evaluation. How do you view yourself? Do you believe that you are important? Do you believe that you are valuable to others?

The opinion of others and the approval of others can hinder us from achieving what we are destined to achieve. When we seek approval and guidance from external factors we begin to lose sight of the true greatness we possess. We lose sight of how important we are, and we allow them to convince us that we have little value. Comparing ourselves to other people only limits and restricts us from embracing our uniqueness which then decreases our self-worth. It's like comparing a real $100 bill to a counterfeit $100 bill. If you don't know the difference between the two, the value placed on the one that's real will not amount to it's true worth. In order to know what's real, you have to know what's real. One morning, as I sat in the parking lot of a manufacturing company waiting to interview for a wellness coordinator position, I called my dad and expressed to him how uncomfortable I was feeling. I told him I didn't like the energy I was receiving as I drove around looking for a place to park. Even though it was a beautiful day, the outside of the building looked cold and lifeless. I looked around and saw hundreds of parked cars, and I felt as though I was pulling into a graveyard. The energy of the environment did not sit well with my spirit. I knew inside the building were hundreds of people working just a job and missing opportunities to live out their purpose. In my eyes, those people were trapped inside and were spending their precious time working beneath their potential. All for the sake of helping someone else achieve their goals and dreams. I couldn't help but feel an energy of imprisonment.

The thought of driving to the same place at the same time every day and performing the same tasks for hours on end for someone else's advancement reminded me that my life would look more like a sentence of imprisonment instead of a sequence of experiences. I had just left a job a few days before with the sole purpose of devoting more time to self-growth, development and living in my purpose. Yet, here I was walking towards a new facility that would once again place restraints on me and prevent me from doing what I was created to do and being who I was created to be. As I expressed my concerns to my dad and the feeling that I wasn't meant to be there, he asked me if I knew how federal agents were trained to recognize counterfeit money. He pulled the following quote from John MacArthur's *Reckless Faith*. "Federal agents don't learn to spot counterfeit money by studying the counterfeits. They study genuine bills until they master the look of the real thing. Then when they see the bogus money they recognize it." He was telling me this to give me a mental picture and help me truly understand how to make the right decision. You can't walk around focusing all your attention on society's limitations, other people's expectations of you, your own unrealistic expectations of yourself, or your own doubts and fears. When you choose to devote your time to becoming who other people expect you to become and doing what other people expect you to do, you're choosing to study the counterfeits of life. You can't know what is real for you when you allow other people to define your realness. Centering your life around the opinions of others is like studying counterfeit bills. How will you know who you are and what you were created to accomplish if you don't take the time to study yourself? There's only one real version of yourself, and that version is very valuable. However, your true value won't be realized until you decide to redirect your attention from the external counterfeits of life back to the internal truths of yourself. Look inside yourself and realize that you are important. Then begin living a life that reflects your true value.

Again I say, in order to know what's real, you have to know what's real. You must examine yourself to discover your true value. You must examine yourself to discover how to truly love yourself. You must examine yourself to discover what it is you want in life. You must examine yourself to discover your purpose. You must examine yourself to discover what makes you happy. Once you have the answers to these questions, you won't allow the counterfeits of life to deceive you. You will begin to experience uneasy energy surrounding you each time you consider settling for something beneath your value. This will become apparent in all aspects of life, your relationships, your job, your spent time, etc. Knowing your truth and knowing what's real for you will serve as a personal guide for your life. International best-selling author, Bryant McGill sums it all up with this one quote: "Real transformation requires real honesty. If you want to move forward -- get real with yourself."

BREAK OUT

"Real transformation requires real honesty. If you want to move forward -- get real with yourself." -Bryant McGill

How many times have you wanted to "break out"? What is it that you've wanted to "break out" of? Do you want to break out of a negative relationship with a friend or a family member? Do you want to "break out" of the restraints of stress placed on you daily by your job? Do you want to "break out" of a religion or religious belief that you no longer believe in or agree with? Do you want to "break out" of an abusive relationship with a significant other? Do you want to break out of a bad habit that is negatively impacting your health and your relationships with the people who love you? As you contemplate your answers and reflect on your experiences, what is it that you feel in these moments of wanting to break out? Are you angry, frustrated, stressed, sad, or depressed? How do you feel when you discover your friend or a family member has lied to you, insulted you, or betrayed you? How do you feel when your alarm clock goes off every morning as a blaring reminder that you have to get out of your cozy bed only to devote anywhere from eight to twelve hours of your life performing repetitive, unfulfilling tasks for the advancement of someone else's company on a daily basis? How valuable is an hour of your life? Are you content with an hour of your life being worth $16.95? What about $8.85? Is one hour of your life more valuable to you than $9.00 or is that what you believe you're worth? How do you feel when the people who are devoted to a religion neglect to love you for the person you are because they're more focused on your "sins", "shortcomings", "wrongdoings", or "imperfections"? How do you feel when your spouse or significant other abuses you physically, emotionally, or both as a means of controlling your life? Are you satisfied with keeping your spirit bird caged because they have convinced you that abuse expresses love? How do you feel when you look in the mirror and you see yourself making excuses for an addicting habit that you're ashamed of, you know is unhealthy, and is causing pain to yourself and the people in your life who care about you? These are examples of prisons that people choose to remain in. More often than not, people decide to stay, not necessarily because they are afraid to leave, but more so because they are afraid of the unknown that lies outside of their cell block. We are all living a life that has an expiration date on it. The body that your spirit dwells in is not meant to last forever. The question is, are you seriously willing to allow the time to run out on your existence before you escape from your personal prisons?

There's a new form of entertainment that has come on the scene in recent years. Many of you may have heard of Breakout Games. On the homepage of the company's website, you'll find the following:

"This isn't your average outing or everyday experience-- breakout is for those who would rather solve mysteries than watch someone else have all the fun. With different rooms that follow unique storylines, you and your friends will have 60 minutes to escape your adventure of choice by cracking codes, solving puzzles and following clues. Part problem solving, part adrenaline, and end-to-end fun."

When I read this description of the game, I'm able to see the colors of life painted across the canvas of the Universe. This isn't a bland existence or cookie cutter experience. Breaking out is for everyone who is looking to discover the divine nature of living in their purpose instead of watching someone else live out their dreams of adventure and unexpected excitement. Breaking out is for everyone who knows there's more to life than doing the same things every day that do not bring them joy. Breaking out is for everyone who is tired of being tired of the current life they live. Breaking out is for everyone who deserves better than what they're currently facing when they wake up each morning. Breaking out is for everyone who looks like you. We live in an age now where you can travel the world without leaving your house. Yes, that's amazing, but what's more beautiful, a tropical bird with illustrious, multi-colored feathers hanging in a cage watching the world from behind a window, or the simple blue jay flying by that window on its path of enjoyment as it continues to embrace the vast experiences of the world without the confinements of metal bars? Both are beautiful in their own light, but one is sitting in a cage while the other is exploring the joys of living a fulfilled life. With different talents and gifts that can guide you down the path of your unique journey, you will begin to realize everything you need to escape your personal limitations is already planted inside of you... if you're willing to tap into it. Life is meant to be filled with adventure and excitement. You have the power to choose how you want to live your life. This is your life, and it's your time to embrace every moment of your journey as the adventure it was meant to be. To take action, you must first make a decision. To live a rich fulfilling life, you have to transform your mindset.

Change vs. Transformation

It's important that you understand, changing your mindset is not enough, you must also seek to transform your mind. Not only do you need to encourage yourself to alter your thoughts, but you also need to change the character and nature of your thinking. Here's a simple example that will help you understand what I'm saying. When someone decides they are tired of coming home to the same leaking gutters, the same busted shutters and the same worn out, run down, stain spotted carpet, they formulate a plan to either change or transform their living space. They begin imagining how their house could look if they installed new carpet, made the necessary repairs, and replaced the things that no longer are of any use or value to them. Next, they begin thinking about what they need to do to make it all happen. Let's pause here for a moment and dig a little deeper into change vs. transformation. Say you decide today that you no longer like the way your house looks. We'll focus on one room. You want your living room to have a homier, more serene feeling too it. Currently the furniture doesn't match, to say the least. You have a burnt orange lazy-boy sitting next to an old futon you purchased from the thrift store that you've had since college. Your carpet appears to be a tannish-brown with questionable freckles, and if anyone decides to slide the lazy-boy 2 inches to the right, you'll remember the carpet was more of a spotless, eggshell white when you first moved into the home. Your 52-inch flat screen TV is mounted so professionally on top of a black, dusty, three-drawer Sterilite cart that is missing the back left wheel. Your curtains look like bed sheets, and the only dependable light source in the room is a five-foot-tall floor lamp slouched over in the corner with a single 40-watt light bulb. Now you have two options. You can change your living room or transform your living room. Let's discuss the differences, shall we? Should you choose to simply change your living room, you could find yourself in the same room with different furniture. Here's how that would look. You would go out and purchase another orange lazy-boy, another futon, the same colored eggshell white carpet, another Sterilite cart (I imagine you'd outdo yourself this time by purchasing one with four sturdy wheels instead of three and five drawers), and another five foot tall lamp with a 60-watt light bulb, because the 40-watt bulb just wasn't satisfying you anymore. That's all well and good, but when all the changes have been made and you sit back to enjoy the much-anticipated feeling of serenity that you knew these changes would bring, you discover that you're still in the same space. Yes, the things in the room have changed, but the room hasn't changed, and that warm, inviting feeling you were seeking is still missing. Why is the peaceful feeling you so anxiously anticipated after changing the furniture in your room not how you imagined? It's because all you've done is changed the room, but you didn't transform the room. Now, let's imagine what transforming the same room would look like. Instead of looking to replace your furniture with furniture that's similar to what you've familiarized yourself with from the past, you decide to do things a little differently. You take the risk of stepping outside of your comfort zone and face the fear that's held you in it for so long. You begin driving around to different hardware stores, or searching online, to get new ideas on ways to improve your home. Heck! You may even hire a home decor specialist to create a new space for you based on your expressed desires. It does require a commitment to invest more effort, time, and money, but you will soon realize it is all worth it. Here's a little nugget I heard listening to one of Dr. Joe Dispenza's interviews. "Taking time in your life to invest in yourself is to invest in the future." Your new space is everything you ever wanted and even more peaceful and inviting than you imagined it would be. You have a chandelier instead of a floor lamp, your TV is now mounted securely on a wall, you have a full living room set equipped with two stylish end tables, your windows are draped with long, luxurious curtains and you're now able to appreciate the beautiful hardwood floors that were once hidden beneath your freckled carpet. As you sit in your new space, you take a deep breath, let it out slowly, and you submerge yourself in the warm, inviting energy as the room embraces you with its peace. That, my friend, is the difference between change and transformation. The dimensions and the structure of the living room didn't change, but the energy and the atmosphere of the living room transformed the room into a completely different space. It does us no good to break off a relationship with someone we called a friend because they lied or betrayed us only to go befriend someone else who does the same things. It does us no good to leave an abusive relationship with one person only to find ourselves in an abusive relationship with a different person. It does us no good to stop one addictive bad habit that has a negative impact on our health and well-being only to replace it with another addictive behavior. It does us no good to walk away from one job only to accept another one that requires the same long hours, the same high stress and the same low pay. Change alone is not always as beneficial as one might think. That is why it is very important to focus on transformation. There's a verse in the Bible that reads: "Be not conformed to this world, but be ye transformed by the renewing of your mind..." Everything that ever was, everything that is, and everything that ever will be are only so because it started in someone's mind. How powerful is that? Our minds have the ability to make us see things that aren't in front of us, hear things when there is no sound, and feel things without being touched. You can watch a nest of spiders hatching and scattering about on television and all of a sudden your mind has convinced you that the tickle on the back of your neck is a spider crawling on you. If the mind is powerful enough to do that, then it is powerful enough to be limitless. Freedom doesn't come from being content sitting within the same cell walls days after day.

Change doesn't occur unless an action has been taken. Breaking out is two-fold. It requires thinking differently, and it requires transforming your mind. Both of which can only occur if some form of action has been taken. Every day is a new day, and every day you are given an opportunity to make choices that can either lead you into your greatness or keep you confined in your personal prison cell of life. I challenge you to break out of your cell, look within yourself, discover your light and use that light to guide you to a life of freedom.

Is your life a sequence of experiences or a sentence of imprisonment?

There are multiple definitions of the word "life" in the dictionary, but there are two in particular that I would like to share with you today. One definition reads: "the sequence of physical and mental experiences that make up the existence of an individual". Another definition reads: "a sentence of imprisonment for the remainder of a convict's life." I don't know about you, but that first definition definitely carries a sweeter tune than the second one. How many days pass without you acknowledging and embracing the experiences of your existence? What color are the leaves on that tree you walk by every day on your way to your car? Are they the same color as they were yesterday? What was the name of your server when you stopped to get a cup of coffee this morning? Did your server have brown eyes, green eyes, or blue eyes? What energy was your spouse giving off when you left the house this morning? Was your spouse happy, sad, excited, or depressed? Did

34

you acknowledge your spouse's energy and provide an appropriate response to it, or did you dismiss and hurry out the door? Most of us live a routine life. We wake up on the same side of the bed, we perform the same morning routine, we leave our house around the same time, and we arrive to work around the same time. We have conditioned ourselves to believe that we know everything about our immediate environments and daily encounters. This conditioning may cause us to miss out on the subtle differences each day brings, and thus miss out on the quiet joys that lie within those subtleties. We miss out on the beauty of life's experiences. That tree we pass every morning, we can assume what color the leaves are depending on the season. But what if, tomorrow, instead of assuming you know what color the leaves are, you take the time to look at that tree? You might discover a new blossom on that tree, or maybe even a bird's nest that wasn't there the day before. What if, instead of impatiently waiting on of your server at your favorite coffee shop, you take the time to look at him or her? You might discover that your server is having a rough morning, and you could be the shift in that person's day with a simple gesture such as a hug or a smile. What if, instead of assuming you "know" how your spouse feels as you're rushing out the door to work, you take a moment to look at him or her? You might discover that your attention to details at that moment is more important than rushing to the red light down the street. Our lives are a series of choices amid a series of events. What we choose in each moment of each day will determine if we're living a life of experiences or if we're simply existing in a self-constructed prison cell.

I will repeat the first part of the second definition. Life is a sentence of imprisonment. How heavy is that? As you sit there thinking about the abusive relationship you're still in, the harmful habits you're still addicted to, or the job you hate but continue to wake up and go to everyday, do you feel like a prisoner? I used to be there. I've experienced all the above, and all along in my heart and mind, I knew that there was always something better for me.

The Relationships

"If you don't like the road you're walking, start paving another one." – Dolly Parton

When we hear the word relationship we automatically assume we're referring to a relationship with a spouse or significant other. Relationships are a connection between us and other people. I've never been in a physically abusive relationship, but some of my past relationships were not healthy. If the relationship is not healthy, then it's unhealthy. If a person is feeling misused in a relationship, then it is my belief that person is being abused. I didn't acknowledge my relationships as being "abusive", but as I look back I realize my value was not being acknowledged or respected. I do not put all the blame on the other people, because I played a role in that too. When you don't see and truly understand your own value, it makes it easier for others to ignore or dismiss it as well. I believe many people, men, and women, are or have been in an abusive relationship, but may not recognize it as such. Abusive can be defined as: "using harsh, insulting language; using or involving physical violence or cruelty; characterized by wrong or improper use of action" (Merriam Webster). When someone disrespects you by using harsh words when speaking to you, that's abuse. When you're in a relationship with someone and that person constantly dismisses your feelings and concerns as it pertains to the nature of the relationship, that's abuse. If you're afraid to communicate your dislikes to your partner, friend, companion, spouse, supervisor, or family member because you're afraid he or she may react in an explosive or harsh insulting tone, that's abuse. When someone threatens to hurt you in any capacity if you decide to walk away, that's abuse. I've held onto relationships with people far longer than I ever should have because I lacked one major quality, unconditional self-love. Once you love yourself, the totality of your existence, you will not allow yourself to settle for anything that does not reflect your value. You won't allow yourself to keep that "friendship", that job or that significant other because you realize that doing so is causing more self-harm than good.

The Addiction

"What characterizes an addiction? Quite simply this: you no longer feel that you have the choice to stop. It seems stronger than you. It also gives you a false sense of pleasure, pleasure that invariably turns into pain." - Eckhart Tolle

I will start off by saying that I have never experimented with or been addicted to any prescription or what they call recreational drugs. However, contrary to what people want to believe or admit, there are plenty of other things to be addicted to, both healthy and unhealthy. You can be addicted to pornography. You can be addicted to receiving attention or sympathy so you do things intentionally to cause physical harm to yourself. You can be addicted to watching television. You can be addicted to social media. You can be addicted to alcohol. You can be addicted to many things. One of the most unrecognized addictions, in my opinion, is the addiction to a sparkly, little, white substance known as sugar. Many people are addicted to sugar. Some of them realize it and others don't. There have been several studies conducted to determine the effects of sugar on the human body. These studies have found that sugar contains similar addictive properties to crack cocaine. How many of you have started a new year's resolution, a thirty-day challenge, or decided to give up something for Lent and your something of choice was sweets? I'll narrow it down even more to sodas (or "pop" for my readers up North). You made up in your mind that for a certain number of days, you would not consume any carbonated sugary beverages. You successfully make it through day one without even looking at a soda. Days two and three are a bit of a struggle, but you pull through those like a champ! You wake up on day four feeling accomplished and motivated, but sometime between day four and day five something starts happening. Your body begins to express to you that it wholeheartedly does not agree with the decision you made to cut out sodas. A little after lunch your head begins to throb without warning. You're trying to concentrate on your work, but your head keeps pounding harder and harder. You tough it out because you don't want to take a sick day. By the time you make it home, you don't want to be bothered by anyone or anything. You just want to pop some medicine to relieve the pain and lay down. Unfortunately for you, your body has different plans. You wake up the next day and your head is throbbing even more intensely than the day before. At some point, you realize the reason your body is freaking out on you is because you're depriving it of its wants. Your body is behaving like a child throwing a temper tantrum in the grocery line because the parent refuses to buy a candy bar. Your body is throwing a temper tantrum to get your attention because it's craving that soda. Last year, an acquaintance of mine decided she wanted to give up drinking Mountain Dew. That was her fizzy beverage of choice. She told me after a couple of days without them, she began experiencing headaches, and she concluded the headaches were due to her not drinking her daily Dew. What did she do? She decided to revert back to drinking the soda. Her body was literally going through withdrawals because she stopped drinking Mountain Dew. I challenge you to spend some time monitoring yourself this week and identify what you're consuming. Be mindful of what you're watching, what you're listening to, and what you're eating. What are you currently addicted to? Be honest with yourself. It is important that you become transparent with yourself. What addictive habits would you like to change? Are you aware of why you're addicted to those things listed above? (The answer to this question should not be, "because it feels good" or "because I like it". The question is to encourage you to look deeper within yourself and determine what you're distracting yourself from when you participate in your addictive acts.) Do you want to break out of those addictions? What do you think YOU can do to work towards freeing yourself from the prison of your addictions? Looking inside yourself for the key to freedom is not always easy, but in the end, it is ALWAYS worth it.

What addictive habits would I like to change?

What's preventing me from ending these habits?

What steps can I take to help me free myself from these habits?

The Job

*"You see somebody, they show up in an
environment, and they count the hours. They don't
make the hours count." – Inky Johnson*

At the end of 2017, I asked God to give me a sign. I wanted clear guidance on whether or not I should leave my current full-time job to take on a full-time position at my part-time job. I asked for a sign because I wanted to be sure I was making the right choice. When I ask for signs, they usually involve something taking place that wouldn't likely take place. I'll pause right here for a brief moment. I know a lot of people don't believe in signs from God or the Universe or any other being that's bigger than the limitations we place on ourselves. That's okay. We all have the freedom to believe what we want to believe, and we're all unique beings. I believe in signs. They work for me. They're a surefire way for me to communicate with the Divine. What works for some doesn't always work for others. Different strokes for different folks, right? Fast forward to the last month of the year, I received the answer to my request. A position opened up at my part-time job, and they offered it to me. You wouldn't believe the joy I felt when that happened. I wanted to leave my full-time job because I felt it was draining the life out of me, literally. That's a heavy statement, but I stand behind it. I was ready to move on from that career because I knew it wasn't for me. I was there because it was a way for me to pay the bills. A little background for you, a couple of years earlier, I had been offered the full-time position at my part-time job, but I turned it down because I didn't want to take the pay cut. I was more focused on those small pieces of paper than I was on my peace of mind, body, and spirit. I knew this time, it was definitely time for me to move on. The circumstances lined up perfectly, and I would not let that opportunity pass by again. I now valued peace of spirit more than I valued a piece of paper. I went through the process of completing all the appropriate steps to accept the full-time position once it was officially available. One month went by. Then two. Then three. I wasn't concerned because I knew I was aligned with the Universe, and the time for me to break out wasn't long off. Fast forward a couple of months, and I was still working the same schedule I had been working at the end of 2017. The position I was so sure I would step into was no longer available, not because someone else was hired for it, but because the new hiring team removed the position. Surely you can imagine my disappointment. After all that time, I had finally shifted my priorities to a place where I valued peace more than society's expectations. I was finally able to take a step of faith, but the ground I intended to step on was removed and it left me feeling like I was being teased. I thought I was trotting my little happy self down the right path then whack! I got smacked in the face by one of those low hanging tree limbs. What do I do now? How do I escape? The door of opportunity is now locked. I knew I was in a place I didn't want to be, but I wasn't sure where I should go and I wasn't sure how I was supposed to get there. I began passively looking for other opportunities, and eventually, I found a few that seemed interesting enough for me to consider. I even had some recruiters reaching out to me for jobs I hadn't even applied for. I thought for sure that was the escape route, so I entertained it with much enthusiasm. One recruiter and I had some good conversations. However, after about a week or so, communication died down. It had gotten to a point where I began to doubt that the opportunity was truly for me. There I was reviewing my current situation and the effects it was having on my spirit, my thinking, and my energy. I didn't agree with how I was existing. I didn't agree with the long days and long drives all to assist with fulfilling someone else's dream. One day, on my way to the full-time job I decided "This is it. I've had enough. This job is draining my energy. I'm a happy, joyful, energetic being who loves to feel the sun on my face and move around whenever I choose to without having to request permission from anyone else. I deserve better than this. My light is dimming each day I pull up at that place. Why do I keep subjecting myself to torture? Who does that?" Yes, I had a good long conversation with myself because it was a good long drive to work. After my conversation with myself that day, I decided to take action. I was nervous about the thoughts that were passing through my head, but I knew something had to be done and the only person who could do it was me. So I did something. I printed up my letter of resignation. I didn't resign the same day because I still had some doubts, and I was still fighting with the fear of the unknown, but I realized that the only way to get out of this cage was to break out. And that's exactly what I did. The next day I turned in my letter of resignation. I felt like a huge burden was lifted off of me and I was immediately surrounded by fresh air. I could breathe again!

Let's pause here for a moment. I'm not telling you to go to work tomorrow and quit your job. We all have responsibilities, and we all have different paths. Although our journeys may be different, the destination is always the same, living a life full of peace and joy. It is important that we do not live our lives counting the hours, but instead, we, live our lives doing things that make the hours count. Motivational speaker and author Les Brown posed this series of questions at one of his speaking engagements.

"If you were given 6 more months to live and guaranteed success, what would you do? If you knew for a fact that in 6 months there would be no more life in your body, would you be content and happy showing up for work every day at your current job? Would you keep postponing that trip that you've been saying you would take for the past three years but kept coming up with reasons why it was never a good time to go? Would you keep neglecting your family because "the bills have to be paid"? What would you do? How would you live your life knowing that 6 months from today you would be but a memory?"

Take a moment to complete this simple exercise on the back of this page. In the left-hand column, write down the reasons why you think you can't break out. In the right-hand column, write down how you will feel and who will benefit when you DO break out.

Why I can't break out   Benefits of breaking out

Now that you have everything written down, review your lists carefully. Once you have reviewed them, take your pen and draw a large 'X' through the left-hand column. Understand that everything you wrote in the left-hand column represents the bars of limitations and self-restrictions. Scribble through that column and don't allow yourself to give it any more attention or energy. You already know what's there, so there's no need to acknowledge it anymore. You've dwelled on it long enough, and now it's time to consider your possibilities. It's time to play in your imagination. It's time to go back to being that little boy or little girl in the fourth grade who got caught staring out the window and daydreaming. You see, you have the choice to move towards your destination, and you have the choice to remain stagnant in your situation. In one of his speeches, Bob Proctor said, "The life of anyone who chooses to live with extreme caution will never amount to anything more than a succession of dull, soporific days, continuing on, without interruption." Don't live a life based on decisions made out of fear. I urge you to break out of your cell and run towards your destination, your true calling. I urge you to live free.

LIVE FREE

"You owe yourself something. Go be free. Go see what God got for you." -
Steve Harvey

What does it mean to live free? When I think of freedom, I think of being surrounded by fresh air, an endless peace, and the ability to come and go as I please. When I think of freedom, I think of a bird. A bird has the ability to travel wherever it wants to go. It has the ability to leave whenever it wants to leave. It has the ability to build its house wherever it wants to live. A bird chooses its life. It's not bound to the rules of anyone else, and it doesn't stay in one tree out of fear of what it might encounter in a different tree. I'm sure you've heard the question 'are you living or do you just exist?' That question should encourage you to reevaluate how you're spending your time daily. When I was living in the shadows, I was living my life according to the guidelines of society. I sought the typical cookie cutter jobs that required me to dedicate a minimum of 8 hours a day in order to receive a constant check. Besides the 8 hours I served inside the building, I had to also dedicate anywhere from 2-3 hours in my car commuting back and forth from work. We have 24 hours in each day, and I was choosing to give almost half of that 24 hours to helping some major corporation reach its goals while I continued to push my goals to the side. Prior to spreading my wings and taking flight, I worked as an IT support representative for a few years. Every day it was the same routine. I took the same route to work. I parked on the same side of the parking lot. I walked into the same building. I sat at the same desk. I heard the same voices. I helped the same clients. Day after day, this was my life. I know several of you can relate to this. How boring and sad does that sound? As I began to near the end of my prison sentence, I mean near the end of my time with that company, I stepped outside of myself and saw everything I just described. I was walking around the pond just outside of our building, and I was thinking about how unfortunate it was for the fish living in the pond. The water was absolutely disgusting. It was so disgusting, it was nicknamed "goose poop pond". Not only were the fish living in a disgusting environment, but they were also forced to live in a confined environment. They didn't have the option to hop out of the pond and move on to a bigger better living space. They swam back and forth restricted to the same walls every day. As I

50

thought about that, I looked up at the building I chose to drive to everyday and realized that it was nothing more than a giant aquarium for the humans that worked inside. I looked at the building and finally saw the cage. I saw a being larger than myself pull the roof of the building back just as you would the lid of a pet aquarium. As the being pulled the roof off the building, I looked down and observed the environment. What I saw was sad and depressing. Every day, the same people drove to the same place. They sat at the same desk. They walked the same hallways. They took the same route to the bathrooms and vending machines. They talked to the same people. They performed the same movements, listened to the same issues, solved the same problems and complained about the same things. It was as if I was watching a maze full of mice wandering around the same room. It looked so depressing. All of these beautiful spirits from different walks of life, different ages, sizes, shapes, and colors were voluntarily confining themselves to the same lifeless walls, and they were choosing to perform the same repetitive tasks that resulted in the same undesirable stress. It was like watching a guinea pig hop on the same spinning wheel day after day and get nowhere. How is that living? I'll answer that question for you, IT'S NOT! There are too many possibilities and too much world around you for you to hate what you're doing every day or hate where and how you're living. Living involves laughter, adventure, excitement, exposure to new things, and so on. Too many of us are alive, but we're not living. We're not living because we choose not to live, not because we're forced not to live. Some of us are actually afraid of living. We're afraid of seeing what possibilities could become realities if we chose to live free instead of choosing to live in our cages. We've convinced ourselves, or allowed others to convince us, that we're "too old" to change direction in life. We've allowed others to paint the picture of what our life should look like as a result of their failures. We use our children as a safety net (excuse) for not stepping out and attempting to live a life doing what we've always wanted to do. All of these cages are hindering us from our freedom. But what if I told you it's never too late as long as you're still alive? It's never too late to live in your purpose and do what you were created to do.

In June 2017 I went to South Carolina to celebrate with my beautiful younger cousin as she graduated high school. On her graduation cap, she had the words "live free" with a black bird flying out of its cage. She's a brilliant intelligent young lady, and I felt it was in my best interest to ask her what that meant to her. Her response was, "for me, it represented stepping into the freedom to be completely myself and no longer living chained up by what I thought other people expected me to be or even by the unrealistic standard I held myself to". This wisdom is coming from a spirit that hasn't even been walking this earth for 20 years. Do you realize how much self-approval and self-love must be present for you to be bold enough to free yourself from the burden of other people's expectations, limitations, and doubt? Do you realize that knowing who you are, appreciating who you are, and valuing the unique gifts you have to offer the world requires self-examination? When you wake up in the morning and step out into the world, are you stepping out as the light you were created to be or do you step out trying to be who others expect you to be? As long as you're being true to yourself, peace and joy will surround your life. Your light is pure and perfect the way it is. There's no need to try on different lamp shades to please others. We lose ourselves so easily in the murky depths of our own thoughts. Our insecurities and lack of self-worth aren't caused by others. Our insecurities and lack of self-worth are born from the conception of our imagination of other people's opinions and our own unrealistic expectations. We would rather focus our energy on trying to please others and live up to the expectations of others rather than searching inside ourselves to discover what satisfies our soul and brings us true joy. We've somehow convinced ourselves and allowed others to convince us that happiness and peace are luxuries. Why aren't they viewed as necessities? What would your life look like if you committed to living a life centered around doing the things that bring YOU happiness and peace? Do you even know what those things might be? If you do know, what's preventing you from acting on those things and ultimately shifting to a more positive living experience? Are you overlooking how valuable you are? Why do you always choose to put the needs, demands, requests, and expectations of others before your personal needs and desires? You've heard the saying; take care of the home, first. I have a quote I like to share sometimes. To be selfless, you have to be selfish. What I mean by that is, in order for you to continue to meet someone else's needs, requests or expectations, you have to first meet your own needs, requests and expectations. It's quite difficult to assist with keeping another person's cup full when yours is constantly running on E. There's only one thing you can pour from an empty cup, and that's emptiness. Please don't misunderstand what I'm saying. As I said before, we are here to serve others, whether it be performing the tasks on your job, tending to the needs of your family and friends, or getting involved with community service projects at your church, school or in your neighborhood. However, when we lack the ability to see the true value of ourselves or we blatantly ignore it, we are doing ourselves an injustice and as a result, doing an injustice to others. In one of his interviews, international lecturer, researcher, author, and educator Dr. Joe Dispenza said: "knowledge is power, but knowledge about yourself is self-empowerment." Empowerment can be defined as, "the process of becoming stronger and more confident, especially in controlling one's life and claiming one's rights." If you aren't yet aware, you have the right to live a life of freedom. Freedom from society's expectations. Freedom from your family's expectations. Freedom from your own unrealistic expectations. Not only do you have the right to live free, but you also have the power to free yourself. Search within and there you will find the key to happiness, the key to peace, the key to freedom. I encourage you to unlock your cage, take to the sky and live free.

LIVE FREE

God created you on purpose.
Gifted, you are a unique light.
The people around may paint you as worthless,
But your gift, when shared, elevates the world to
great heights.

Deep inside the soul of your earth
Lie the seeds of a greatness yet to take root.
Explore your light as you experience a rebirth.
Life eternal resides inside of you.

Freedom comes at a price
You must be willing to pay.
Why long for freedom in another life
When you can choose freedom today?

The world's tallest tree began first as a seed,
Bold enough to aim for the sky.
Greatness erupts when your gift is freed.
Release yourself from your cage and fly.

Freedom can never be taken from you.
It lives in the heart of your mind.
The limitations perceived reflect your personal
views.
I urge you, Live Free while there's still time.

Emily Hayes

YOU G.O. GIRL! YOU G.O. BOY!

"Get Out of your comfort zone, Gain Optimism, Generate Opportunities, Get Obsessed, Give Often" – Emily Hayes

Get **O**ut of your comfort zone

"A ship is always safe at the shore but that is not what it is built for." – Albert Einstein

What does it mean to get out of your comfort zone? Before we answer that question, let's discuss what a comfort zone is. A comfort zone could be anything that doesn't incite a sense of fear or stress. Merriam

Webster dictionary defines a comfort zone as "the level at which one functions with ease and familiarity". Your comfort zone could be avoiding eye contact when talking to people, avoiding meeting and interacting with people you do not know, going to the same coffee shop, wearing clothing and/or make that hide your insecurities, not speaking in front of a crowd of people, looking down when you walk, combing or cutting your hair a specific way, etc. Another, more dangerous, comfort zone is staying in a negative situation with a fearful mindset. Many times we stay in negative situations, relationships, jobs, living arrangements, etc. because we are familiar with that pain, hurt and dis-ease. We know what to expect when we come home to a roommate that constantly eats our food but never goes grocery shopping. We know what to expect when we stay in a relationship where the other person is abusive. We know what to expect when we return to the same building and deal with the same coworker or supervisor who is constantly talking behind our backs and doing things to set us up for failure. We know what to expect when we walk into the house and our brother or sister's dirty clothes are strewn about, there are empty soda cans all over the kitchen table, and there are three empty cereal boxes in the refrigerator. It sounds strange to voluntarily subject ourselves to those stressors regularly, doesn't it? That's because it is, but we do that because we are in a familiar place. We have a choice to stay or leave. However, we convince ourselves that where we currently are, despite the constant discomfort, pain, negative energy and stress we're experiencing, is safer than the unknown. We find ourselves in a state of being more afraid of what might happen or what we might experience by stepping out into the world of the unknown or trying something different. It seems better and safer to remain in the familiar stressors of our stagnant daily existence. In an interview describing his first skydiving experience, Will Smith said this, "the point of maximum danger is the point of minimum fear. It's bliss. God placed the best things in life on the other side of terror. On the other side of your maximum fear are all the best things in life." Skydiving may be an extreme example but some of us fear getting out of our comfort zone on the same level as someone afraid of heights fears jumping out of a perfectly good airplane. Since the day we were born we've all had to experience the feeling of getting out of our comfort zones. From birth itself to learning how to walk to our first day of school, our first relationship, our first interview, our first job, we've all experienced the uneasiness of stepping out of our comfort zone. But had we not tried we would not be who we are and where we are today. It's important that we don't concern ourselves with what other people may or may not think about us. People are going to think what they want to think regardless of what you do and how you do it. As a matter of fact, those people probably have the same or similar ideas as you but were too afraid to take the chance. Most of us build our comfort zones around other people's opinions or the thought of other people's opinions whether we realize it or not. Isn't that crazy? That just the thought of what someone else may or may not be thinking can completely hinder us from doing something we previously set our heart and mind to do. An apple tree doesn't stop being an apple tree simply because the orange tree produces oranges. Both trees grow and produce their fruits regardless of what the other produces. If we redirect our focus and energy to how great we could be by being our best selves, we could break through the walls of comfort, embrace the momentary discomfort, and jump into the bliss of living, not existing, the life we were created to live.

Take a moment to identify and write down your comfort zone(s).

As I've danced down the vibrant rugged path of my journey, I've learned that my biggest comfort zone was staying in the shadows, hence the title of this book. How did I stay in the shadows, you ask? I would do things to keep attention away from my face, my appearance, and my overall self. Not that I don't like my face. It's actually a pretty cool face. It has bubbly brown eyes, a single black freckle on the left cheek, and a nose and mouth that appear to be centered on most days of the week. Here is one example of how I stayed in the shadows. As I'm still in the early years of establishing a solid foundation for my nonprofit, SERVED, I thought it would be vain to highlight myself when the purpose was to focus on serving others. Many of my friends and people who are very dear to me have been constantly encouraging me to show the people who I am. There were two main limitations (excuses) I would wrap myself in when presented with that advice. The first was that I wanted my nonprofit to be the focus. I wanted the name and the logo to be the "face" of the nonprofit. The second pushback I would give is that I don't like public speaking. Speaking in public and in front of crowds or a camera makes me nervous, as I mentioned before. My face turns red, my voice gets shaky, and my body decides to turn on its natural cooling mechanism without consulting with me first. (For those of you not quite familiar with your natural cooling mechanism, it's called sweating.) Every time I told people that I didn't like public speaking, they would respond by saying they couldn't tell based on the few interviews I've done and our conversations. A few weeks after I began writing this book I realized that constantly saying I wasn't a good public speaker and speaking in front of groups made me nervous, was actually my way of encouraging myself to remain in the shadows (my comfort zone). My comfort zone wasn't the actual shadows or avoiding being in the public eye. My comfort zone was the feeling of anxiousness and fear, the shaky voice, the flushed face, and the nervous sweating. I was comfortable with those side effects of public speaking because I've had them for as long as I can remember, and they are the familiar stressors. Therefore, it was okay for me to be afraid. A good friend of mine shifted my view when he told me that I was focusing more of my attention on myself than the people I created SERVED to help. Talk about a shattered mindset. There I was with a desire to build a successful organization to help others on the foundation of wanting all the attention to be away from me and focused on those in need, only to be shown that I was making decisions that opposed my desires. I wanted everyone else to focus on the needs of others, but at the same time, I was allowing my personal fears and my comfort zones to hinder me from fully focusing on them. I was putting my fears before their needs. I was building speed bumps that were slowing down the process and progress of SERVED reaching its potential.

Getting out of your comfort zone is not only healthy for you, but it is helpful for others. When you get out of your comfort zone, you open up the door to a world of possibilities. You remove the ceilings and limitations hindering you from greatness and living a life full of wonderful experiences. Getting out of your comfort zone shifts the attention from self to helping others and fulfilling your purpose. In one of his speeches, John Rogers said, "When people have the courage to journey to the center of their fear, they find nothing. It is only many layers of fear being afraid of itself." Think about that. Outside of the lines of your comfort zone lies the center of your fear. Inside the center of your fear lies the world of freedom. Freedom from insecurity. Freedom from negative thoughts. Freedom from the job you hate. Freedom from bad relationships. Freedom from suffocating stress. Freedom from poor decisions. Freedom from everything that is holding you back from being the best you that you were created to be. When you decide not to venture outside of your comfort zone, you're choosing to allow your habits, your insecurities and your shame to be a crutch as you hobble along to becoming a lesser version of your true self.

Gain Optimism

"It always seems impossible until someone does it."
– Nelson Mandella

Being optimistic and having a positive outlook or attitude is a choice. When you imagine yourself surrounded by positivity in your mind, it helps you to focus on the choices you make daily when responding to the various situations you encounter. When you strive to be optimistic about your experiences, you'll begin to shift your thinking. Our circumstances have little to do with our fulfillment in life. It's how we approach our circumstance. It's our attitude towards our circumstances that makes the difference. Seeking positivity allows you to focus on the positive aspects that you once overlooked. The opinions you didn't ask for but somehow seem to constantly attract could lead you to solving a problem you've been struggling with for weeks. Having to run back inside to change the pants you split while getting in the car to head to work could've helped you avoid being in that four-car pileup you passed this morning. Maybe that extra talkative coworker, who is completely illiterate when it comes to reading body language and is the source of your weekly Monday morning headaches, is actually playing a major role in helping to temporarily distract you from the throbbing pain of the ankle you sprained over the weekend trying to prove to your middle son that you can still skateboard. All jokes aside, how you respond to your external environment has a major impact on your internal environment. Motivational speaker and best-selling author, John Maxwell said, "Attitude is the paintbrush of the mind". What you think and how you feel is revealed through your emotional responses. When I think about this quote, I immediately think of Bob Ross. For all of my younger readers out there Bob Ross was the best public broadcast televised painter of all time. If you do not know who he is, please YouTube him. Anytime Bob Ross would make a mistake while painting he would take his brush and, as he put it, paint a happy tree over the mistake. That's how we should handle the circumstances that arise in our lives. Despite what we're going through, there's always something beautiful that can come out of it. Next time you face a negative situation in your life, I challenge you to find the happy tree.

The first law of thermodynamics states that energy can neither be created nor destroyed; energy can only be transferred or changed from one form to another. Therefore, the energy that is presented to you cannot be destroyed. It is either transferred directly to you as it is or you change it into something else. Whether it is positive energy or negative energy, you have the power to change it or receive it as it is. You can be in the company of others with a happy spirit and a happy attitude, and in that same space, someone else is walking around in misery. That person sees everything as dark, sad and gloomy. It's like the coworker that shows up to work every day complaining about having to be at work. You look at them, and it's like you can literally see the cartoon storm cloud hovering over them, firing off lightning bolts, and pouring rain on their head. Their face is long, and their energy is sunken. Meanwhile, there you are walking around all bright, vibrant, and happy as if you're the sparkling love child of sunshine and rainbows. You say good morning to everyone and ask them how they're doing. While some people would rather not have to keep showing up to the same job just to earn a check to pay bills, they're still able to respond with a little positivity. You are a source of joy to the space that you are presently in, but not every person will receive your energy. Some people will take your energy, changed it, and turn it into something negative, turn it into something dark, turn it into something gloomy. Keep in mind, you have the exact same choice, and you have to exact same power. Anytime someone approaches you and gives you energy, you can choose to either receive that transferred energy directly as it is or you can change it. You can change it from positive to negative or you can change it from negative to positive. It is up to you.

One of my daily affirmations is "I am everything I need". What I mean when I say that is, everything I need to be successful, everything I need to be happy, everything I need to be valuable is all inside of me. Success, happiness, value, etc. is not dependent on the opinions of others. It's built on the foundation of loving yourself first and always. When you love yourself, you respect yourself. When you respect yourself you don't settle for anything or anyone. The way I see it, you have two options. You can value yourself and believe it until you see it. Or you can allow the naysayers, the pessimists, the negative critiques, destructive criticism, and other negative outside sources to destroy your dreams and imagination until you can no longer see the unique greatness inside of you. I urge you to take charge of your responses, take charge of your outlook, and gain optimism!

Generate Opportunities

"Any idea that is held in the mind, that is emphasized, that is either feared or revered will, begin at once to cloth itself in the most convenient and appropriate form available" - Andrew Carnegie

We live in a world of limitless possibilities. Anything you could ever think of is possible. A lot of things exist today because someone created an opportunity where others didn't see one. Opportunities don't always come to you. You must seek them. And when you feel there aren't any available, it is up to you to create them. Life isn't about doing something once and expecting it to turn out the way you imagined it would. A gardener doesn't poke a hole in the ground place one seed in it and then walk away expecting to yield a full crop. He pokes several holes and plants several seeds.

One weekend I was sitting at the kitchen table having a conversation with a good friend of mine, and he said something very powerful. As soon as I heard it, I picked up my phone and wrote it in my notes because I didn't want to forget it. He said "God created a seed within a seed. A new seed doesn't have to be created. There is abundance and it's within the seed." Everything you need to become everything you were meant to become has already been placed inside of you. You don't have to search outside yourself to find that which is already planted within. The opportunities you need already exist and are waiting for you to water them. Simply put, opportunities are the recipes to possibilities. You are the catalyst of your life. You have the power to create change! If you don't have the key to the door, remove the hinges. If you don't have enough materials to build a bridge, build a boat instead. It's not that we have to think outside the box, but rather, we must realize there is no box. We have to be bold enough to reject the limitations of society. We were born to create. We have to realize that we are no longer in kindergarten and coloring inside the lines no longer applies to us. The most successful people in the world don't see lines. They don't see limitations because greatness does not manifest from limitations. Greatness manifests from possibilities. It manifests from creativity. It manifests from asking yourself "why not ". When someone tells you no, take that N and O, flip them around, and GO ON! Not everyone can see and understand your vision. Not everyone has the desire to understand your purpose. Not everyone possesses the same amount of enthusiasm for your passion. People have landed on the moon. It is clear we have proof that anything is possible. All we have to do is develop our own recipe. What ideas do you have that you haven't acted on because you haven't seen it done before or no one seems to be willing or able to support you? What can you do to create an opportunity for those ideas? Are you waiting to see it in order for you to believe it, or do you believe it's possible therefore you already see it?

Let's see if we can increase the amount of joy in your daily life and get you one step closer to living in your purpose. In the first row, write down three of your ideas or dreams. In the second row, write down what limiting factors have prevented you from turning those dreams into reality. In the third row, list the ways you will begin to create opportunities for yourself that will help you turn those dreams into your reality. (Keep in mind that your possibilities are limitless. The next page should be filled with all the possibilities you can imagine.)

My Ideas/Dreams

My Limitations

How I will create opportunities

.

Get Obsessed

"Obsession is a mystical tale, a vision of things unseen. To the obsessed person, it's a precious gem, but to others concern it may bring. When you journey this life down the path of your purpose, your life is lived to its best. Discover your passion, shine bright your light, live free and get obsessed" – Emily Hayes

Whatever you invest your time and energy in you become good at. When you devote time daily to running, you become a more efficient runner and your mile time decreases. When you devote your time to baking, you become the person everyone recommends when someone needs to get a cake baked for MawMaw's 98th birthday party. When you devote your time to shooting free throws, you become automatic from the free-throw line. When you focus your attention on developing your ideas and shaping your dreams, you will discover your gifts and you will fulfill your life's purpose. What does it take to accomplish anything in life? It takes the will to do it. The same will and determination you had when you were learning how to walk is still in you today. The difference between now and then is that back then you believed there were no limitations. When you were a child and you were determined to get something, you kept attempting to walk until you made it to the object that held your attention. You were obsessed with getting that bottle of milk. You were obsessed with getting those animal crackers. You were obsessed with getting that bowl of cereal. Whatever your parents and family members used to lure you to let go of the couch and step out on your own two feet was enough to convince you that it was worth it. It did not matter how many times you fell, nothing and no one could convince you that you weren't capable or good enough to walk. Let your dreams be that bottle of milk. Let your ideas be those animal crackers. Let your obsession be that bowl of cereal. Want something enough, create a way to get it, and go after it. I said it before, and I will say it again. The only limitations that exist are the ones we place on ourselves. You are too gifted and too talented not to be obsessed with what you have to offer at this world.

Here are a few of my favorite Les Brown quotes.

"Life takes on meaning when you become motivated, set goals and charge after them in an unstoppable manner."

"Your dream was given to you. If someone else can't see it for you, that's fine, it was given to you and not them. It's your dream. Hold it. Nourish it. Cultivate it!"

"The graveyard is the richest place on earth, because it is here that you will find all the hopes and dreams that were never fulfilled, the books that were never written, the songs that were never sung, the inventions that were never shared, the cures that were never discovered, all because someone was too afraid to take that first step, keep with the problem, or determined to carry out their dream."

Give Often

"There is no limit to the amount of good you can do if you don't care who gets the credit" -Ronald Reagan

We are here not only to enjoy the gift of life but to enjoy the gift of others. We cannot enjoy gifts when we choose not to share them. What good is having money in the bank if no one spends it? What good is buying a present for someone, but you never give it to them? Likewise, what good is having talents and gifts if you don't share them with the world? There's something special about you. When you share your light (gifts) with others, the world becomes a better place. Each of you has something that the rest of us need. When you use your gifts to serve others, you are investing in something greater than yourself, and that's when you experience true success. Giving is not limited to money. Giving is an act expressed in many forms. Giving can be expressed in the form of actual gifts, time, talents, services, etc. You know what talents you have. If you are good at knitting, then consider knitting hats to give to chemotherapy patients. If you have your own lawn service, then consider cutting your disabled neighbor's grass. If you're good at baking, then consider baking a couple of batches of cookies and taking it to the senior citizen living facility. If you're good at math, then consider volunteer tutoring at your local library. If you're good at cutting hair, then consider going to your local orphanage and cut the children's hair. Having a positive impact on the world does not require you to travel the world. You can impact the world by starting with your community. Remember every choice you make has an impact on your environment and the people in it. In one of her interviews, Oprah Winfrey said, "Not everyone can be famous, but everyone can be great because greatness is determined by service." If you haven't discovered your gifts yet, you can still give. There are no limitations when it comes to giving. You always have been and you always will be everything you need. When the seasons change and the hats, gloves, and scarves go on clearance at your local department store, you can purchase a couple of pairs to give to the homeless people the following winter. If you feel you have nothing to give, you still have something to give. Are you aware that something as simple as leaving an uplifting note on a stranger's windshield could completely change their entire day? If you can't give something tangible, then give a hug, give a smile, or give an encouraging word. We are here on this planet to serve each other. You are important. Your presence is a gift. Your gift is invaluable, and it needs to be shared.

Lastly, I would like to leave you with Arnold Schwarzenegger's five rules to success.

1. Find your vision and follow it. If you don't have a vision/goal you're just floating around without a purpose

2. Never ever think small. If you're going to accomplish anything, you have to think big; you have to go and shoot for the stars. The biggest challenge most people have is because they think small. The reason why people think small and choose small little goals is because they are afraid to fail... the only time you're considered a failure is if you fall and don't get up, but if you get up, you're never considered a failure.

3. Ignore the naysayers.

4. Work your a** off. You never want to fail because you didn't work hard enough. You can't climb the ladder of success with your hands in your pocket.

5. Don't just take, give something back. Leave your mark on the world. We must serve a cause that is greater than ourselves. In the end, we will be judged not by how much we made, but how much we give. We don't have to work on just me, we must also work on we. To live a truly full life, you must give back. You must leave the world a better place than you found it.

Today, I encourage you to get out of your comfort zone, gain optimism, generate opportunities, get obsessed, and give often. You GO girl! You GO boy!

WITH MANY THANKS

I want to thank you for supporting me on my mission to inspire millions. I hope this book has been a blessing to your life and an inspiration to you. I appreciate you. I appreciate your support. I appreciate your love. You are a blessing to this world. You are a gift to this earth. You are a light, and you were created to shine. Shine bright sweet spirit and live free.

Love, peace, and blessings
Emily Hayes

Daily Affirmations

AFFIRM

1 a : validate, confirm
  b : to state positively

2 a : to show or express a strong belief in or
dedication to

Daily Affirmations allow you to begin to visualize and
create the focus of the things you want to see in your
life. Affirmations are the GPS of your life experience.
The words you speak daily are directing your life to a
specific destination. When you intentionally focus your
thoughts on that which you desire, you become more
and more aware of those things in your daily
experiences. Think of it this way. When you
purchased your new car, you were very happy. It
brought about a feeling of joy. In the days following
your purchase, you began noticing other people
driving "your car". It's not that the cars weren't on the
road before; it's that you became more aware of them
now because your new car is your new focus. The
same principle is applied to affirmations. It's not that
what you desire, whether it be happiness, peace,
financial stability, etc., doesn't already exist because it
does. You simply need to alter your mindset and shift
your focus to those desires, and you will begin to see
them manifest in your life.

I encourage you to speak peace, love, positivity, and blessings over your life daily. (Be sure to speak them in the present tense.) Here are a few affirmations you can speak daily to get you started. Use the remaining space to write your personal affirmations.

I am strong.

I am healthy.

I live in peace and gratitude.

I am limitless.

I am important.

I love myself.

I love others.

I am everything I need.

Beyond the Shadows

FREEDOM TO EMBRACE THE LIGHT WITHIN

ABOUT THE AUTHOR

Alabama native, Emily Hayes, is a poet, author, artist, fitness enthusiast, founder of a nonprofit organization, lover of life, and most importantly, a light in this world. She loves animals and being out in nature. Emily believes the connection between spirit, mind, and body is essential to enjoying your life experience. She is passionate about serving others and is on a mission to inspire millions.

33017922R00055